MY CHRISTMAS ACTIVITIES

Name _____

Colour in one bauble every time you complete an activity.
When you complete the final activity, colour in the star and the tree!
(Pencils and crayons are work best for this book)

Colour me in!

ROBIN

My robin's name is _____

Christmas wordsearch

Can you find the words hidden in the square?

```
S A N T A S P C R
T R E E S T R O U
O I T N L A E O D
C R O F E R S K O
K A Y O I W E I L
I F S M G I N E P
N F Y C H E T S H
G E L V E S N O W
O R N A M E N T W
```

Santa	stocking	snow	toys
elves	tree	cookies	ornament
Rudolph	star	present	sleigh

Design Santa's sack!

Christmas coordinates

Write the coordinates of each Christmas icon
(*We've added Santa's!*)

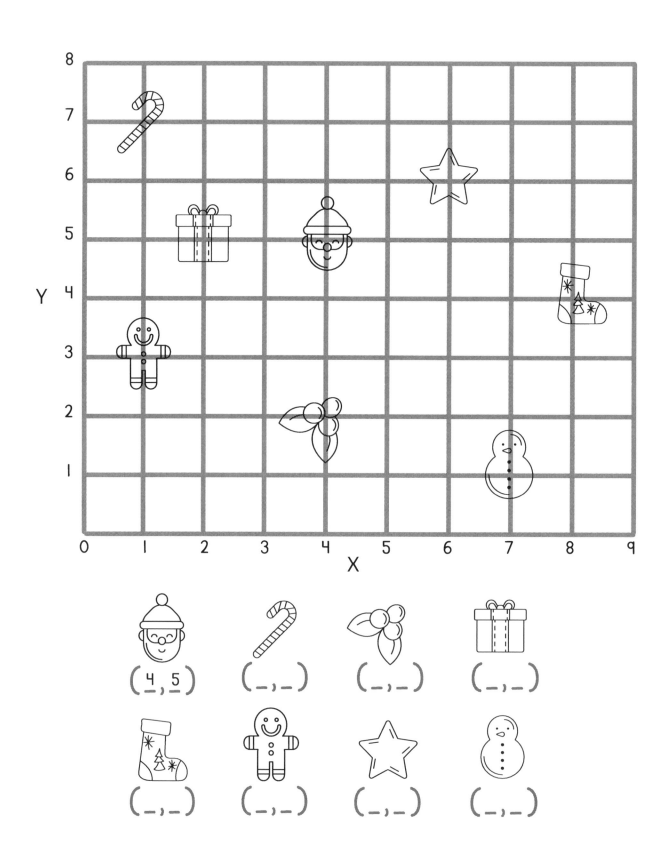

(4 , 5) (_ , _) (_ , _) (_ , _)

(_ , _) (_ , _) (_ , _) (_ , _)

Connect the dots from 1 to 100 and colour in!

Colour me in!

PENGUIN

My penguin's name is _____

Copy me!

Practise your drawing by copying each of these
Christmas pictures in the box provided.
You can colour them all in!

Christmas is scrambled up!

Unscramble these Christmas words, and draw one
of the items underneath

TASNA

_____

ERTE

_____

REEEDRIN

_____

SWNMOAN

_____

TSRA

_____

Trace and colour

Trace the dotted lines and then colour in the picture!

Christmas maze

Can you help Santa find his sleigh?

Colour and count

Can you colour in and count how many there
are of each Christmas picture?

Colour me in!

REINDEER

My reindeer's name is _____

Copy me!

Practise your drawing by copying each of these
Christmas pictures in the box provided.
You can colour all of them in!

Christmas Grid

Use the grid to help you copy the Christmas image.

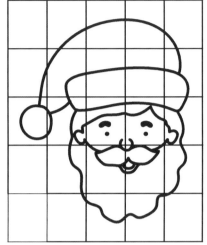

Which stocking?

Use a different colour for each candy cane and follow the path to find which stocking it belongs to then colour in the stocking and candy cane to match!

Colour me in!

SNOWMAN

My snowman's name is _____

Colour and count

Colour and count the Christmas images in each box, and then circle the correct number!

8   7   9   6

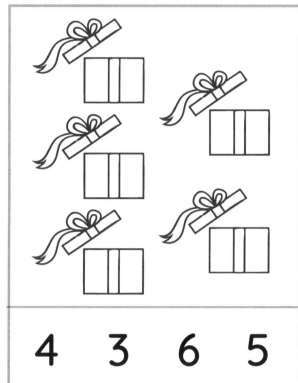

4   3   6   5

5   4   3   6

2   3   8   7

Design a Christmas jumper!

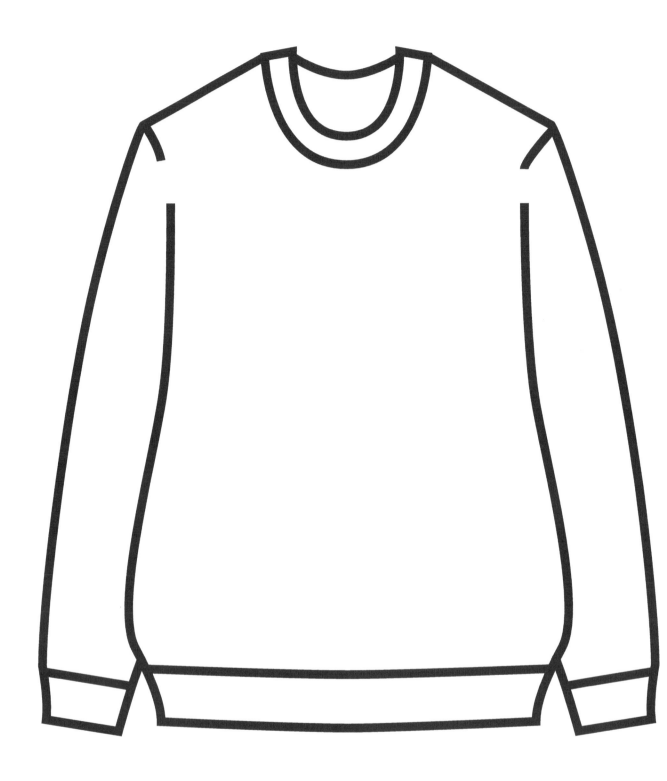

Trace and colour

Trace the dotted lines and then colour in the picture!

Christmas maze

Can you help the snowman find his hat?

Connect the dots from 1 to 53 and colour in!

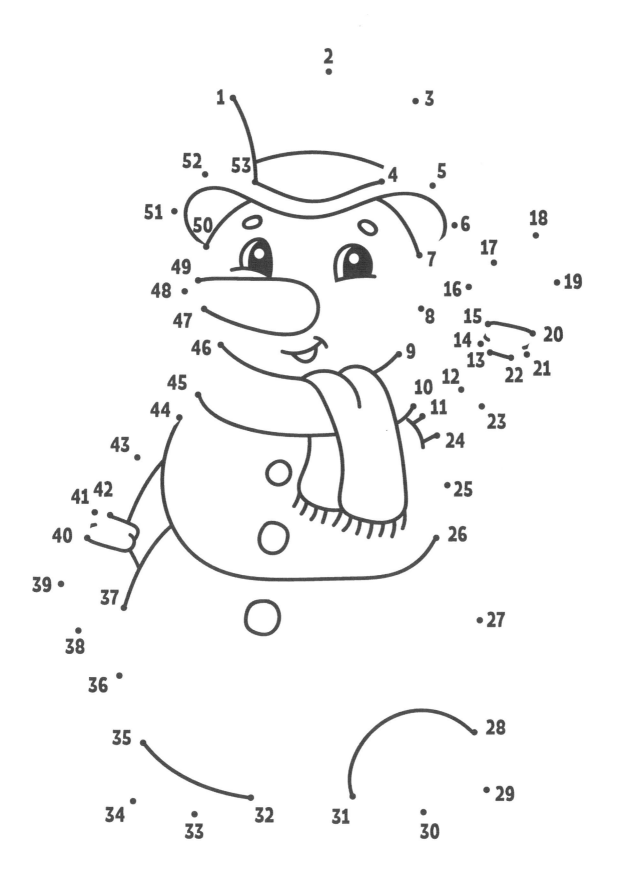

Where's the other half?

Use the grid to draw the other half of this hat and then colour it in!

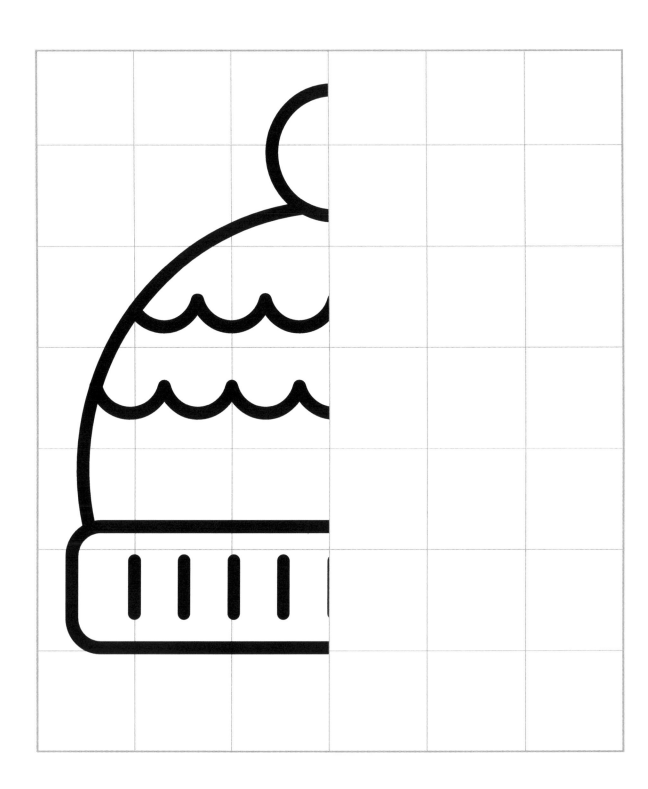

What am I?

Draw a line to join the picture to the word and then write a sentence that includes one of the items, or colour them all in.

Holly

Stocking

Hat

Candy cane

Angel

Gift

_____

_____

_____

You've completed your
Christmas countdown!

We hope you have a
lovely Christmas!

For more Acorns to Oaks products and information,
please visit www.linktr.ee/acornstooaks
or scan the QR code below:

Printed in Great Britain
by Amazon

27961688R00018